to

_____

from

_____

May this little book bring you joy . . .

and the inspiration to give this Christmas away . . .

this holiday season and all year long.

101
simple & thoughtful
ways to
give this
Christmas
away

MATTHEW WEST

Tyndale House Publishers, Inc.
Carol Stream, Illinois

Visit Tyndale's exciting Web site at www.tyndale.com.

Visit www.givethischristmasaway.com for more ways to give this Christmas away.

Visit Matthew West's Web site at www.matthewwest.com.

TYNDALE and Tyndale's quill logo are registered trademarks of Tyndale House Publishers, Inc.

Give This Christmas Away

Designed by Dean H. Renninger

Edited by Bonne L. Steffen

Published in association with the literary agency of Fedd and Company Inc., 9759 Concord Pass, Brentwood, TN 37027.

Library of Congress Cataloging-in-Publication Data

West, Matthew.
    Give this Christmas away / Matthew West.
        p. cm.
    ISBN 978-1-4143-3644-2 (hc)
    1. Christian life—Miscellanea. 2. Christmas—Miscellanea. 3. Charity—Miscellanea. I. Title.
    BV4509.5.W433   2009
    241'.4—dc22
                                                    2009035470

Printed in Canada

15 14 13 12 11 10 09
7   6   5   4   3   2   1

"GIVE THIS CHRISTMAS AWAY"

What if I told you, you have the power
To give someone hope far beyond their wildest dreams.
What if I told you, it's right there in your hands, in your hands.
It's hard to imagine how something so small
Could make all the difference, tear down the tallest wall.
What if December looked different this year?

What if we all just give this Christmas away
If there's love in your heart, don't let it stay there.
Give this Christmas away
And your life will be changed by the gift you receive,
When you give this Christmas away.

It's feeding the hungry, serving the poor,
It's telling the orphan, You're not forgotten anymore.
It's doing what love does even when no one's watching you.
For God so loved the world that He gave us all His Son,
So we could be his hands, his feet, his love . . . his love.

What if we all just give this Christmas away
If there's love in your heart, don't let it stay there.
Give this Christmas away
And your life will be changed by the gift you receive,
When you give this Christmas away.

INTRODUCTION
A DIFFERENT KIND OF LIST

I still make a list. Been doing it since I was a kid. Around Thanksgiving I begin making my Christmas wish list in the hopes that there will be no surprises waiting for me under the tree. Let's be honest: no one wants to say on Christmas morning, "Oh, this is great! I've always wanted a Chia Pet." Like I said, no surprises. These days I hand the list to my wife and drop hints to the rest of my family (complete with Web addresses for purchasing the gifts). After all, the key to making a Christmas wish list foolproof is eliminating the guesswork.

My list usually consists of some things I need but mostly stuff that I want and never got around to buying. Regardless, every year all the items have one common thread: it's all about me. I'm pretty certain I'm not the only list-carrying member of the "ME club" at Christmastime. Each year, after receiving all the things on my list, I find myself coming to the same conclusion: the things we are convinced will satisfy the longings deep within us only leave us wanting more.

Recently I was asked to write a song for the end credits of the VeggieTales Christmas movie *Saint Nicholas - A Story of Joyful Giving*. This movie's message is clear: true joy can be found at Christmas when we give. And we can give because God has given so much to us. To further help spread that message, VeggieTales has teamed up with Operation Christmas Child (OCC), a project started by Franklin Graham that shows how to give big. As the 2008 spokesperson for OCC, I am proud to say that across the country we collected over eight million shoe boxes filled with toys and other items—gifts for children around the world who would not have had a Christmas otherwise.

The song "Give This Christmas Away" was inspired by the VeggieTales movie and the work of OCC. Throughout the songwriting process, I kept circling around the line "What if December looked different this year?" My hope was to write more than a catchy tune. I wanted to create something that could shift our gift-giving attitudes this Christmas by challenging us to think of the needs of others. This is where the book *Give This Christmas Away* comes in. It not only encourages you to give but also provides you with a list of creative and unique ways to do it. It's a different kind of Christmas list.

In addition, we have created a Web site—www.givethischristmasaway .com—where you can add to this giving list by sharing the different ways you have found to give to others. We've also posted links on the Web site to organizations that we feel capture what the spirit of giving looks like. Check out the organizations and see how you can get involved. My hope is that the spirit of giving will be found not only at Christmas but each and every day of the year. It's a small way of giving thanks for the most precious gift that humanity has ever received—Jesus Christ, our Immanuel, God with us: "For God loved the world so much that he gave his one and only Son" (John 3:16). Christmas celebrates God's gift to each one of us. Will you help make December look different this year?

—*Matthew West*

❄ **1** ❄

Take a second look at that old shoe box.

Who would have thought a shoe box could bring so much joy? Operation Christmas Child (OCC) has found a way for shoe boxes to change the lives of countless children all across the world. Last year I had the honor of being a spokesman for their amazing cause. And together, we collected over eight million shoe boxes filled with things like toys, toothbrushes, and school supplies. Operation Christmas Child delivers those gifts to children who would otherwise have no Christmas. A shoe box filled in Chicago could end up reaching a child in Russia. On a recent trip to Bogotá, Colombia, I witnessed firsthand the far-reaching impact of OCC and the power of something as small as a shoe box. The children who received these boxes were smiling from ear to ear, as if they'd just been given the gift of hope. In a way, that's exactly what they had been given.

Join Operation Christmas Child this year in their effort to bring Christmas to millions of children. In addition to receiving your gift, each child is also given a special message about the greatest gift of all, the love of Christ. So by simply packing a shoe box, you are opening up a door to change a child's life for eternity. For parents, this is an effective way to begin teaching your children what Christmas is all about.

> *Learn to do good. Seek justice. Help the oppressed. Defend the cause*
> *of orphans. Fight for the rights of widows.*
> ISAIAH 1:17

Hold the door.

It's a battlefield out there. Sure there may be some sappy elevator music version of "Silver Bells" playing throughout the five-level department store, but don't let it fool you. The shopping malls at Christmas can be downright war zones, and it's every man for himself. (That's why when my wife forces me to go with her to the mall I usually camp out at the food court.) I suggest we change our tactics—show some kindness this Christmas by being aware of the little things. See the woman with three kids in tow walking into the store behind you? Stop and hold the door open for her and her small troop.

· This kind of thoughtfulness can be contagious. There's a good chance that woman will extend the favor to someone else somewhere down the line. If you're in a hurry, this will be a good way to slow yourself down. And even if that woman you were courteous to grabs the very last Elmo Live! before you do, the world's not going to come to an end. Can I get an Amen?

The seeds of good deeds become a tree of life.
PROVERBS 11:30

❄ **3** ❄
Give thanks.

This Christmas, try practicing a continual attitude of thankfulness. Just as the words of the old hymn say, "Count your blessings, name them one by one. Count your many blessings, see what God hath done." Write them down if you need to. I think you'll see that none of us have a shortage of things to be thankful for.

In fact, I believe we are called to be thankful for our problems, too. This is a lesson I have learned firsthand over the years, and I have experienced the transformation that takes place when my perspective on a problem shifts from troubled to thankful. As you give thanks even for your problems, you are saying to everyone around you, "God is at work in the midst of my difficulties and obstacles." I know it sounds crazy. I mean, who in his or her right mind thanks God for the loss of a job? Imagine someone praying, *Thanks, God, for this illness that has taken away all of my strength.* It sounds unnatural, doesn't it? If you find yourself facing a trial this Christmas, thank God for your problems. Thank him for the promise that he will "never leave you nor forsake you." Thank him in advance for what he will do in your life and in the lives of others through this difficulty.

Let your lives overflow with thanksgiving for all he has done.
COLOSSIANS 2:7 (TLB)

❄ 4 ❄
Write a letter.

I should have written that letter. My grandmother's health was fading, and I knew she wouldn't be here on earth much longer. Many times it had crossed my mind to write and tell her how much she meant to me. She had written so many encouraging notes to me. But I would get caught up in something and another day would go by with my feelings untold. Then on New Year's Day 2009 we received the phone call that Grandma West had gone to be with the Lord. Immediately my heart sank. *The letter. I never wrote that letter.* Nearly a year later, I still regret not getting it done; I always will.

Can you think of someone you know who deserves to hear just how much they mean to you? Don't wait until it's too late. When it comes to mind, drop whatever you're doing. And forget e-mail. Turn off your cell phone. A text message doesn't cut it. Go old school on this one. Pick up a pen and paper. I don't care if your handwriting looks like chicken scratch. Write a letter this Christmas to someone you love, to someone you respect. The recipient will cherish that letter always, just like I cherish the letters my grandmother wrote to me.

The words of the godly are a life-giving fountain.
PROVERBS 10:11

❄ **5** ❄
Hit a home run this Christmas.

Albert Pujols is considered by many to be Major League Baseball's best player. The St. Louis Cardinals first baseman was Rookie of the Year in 2001, MVP two times, and a World Series champion. In the world of sports, Albert is larger than life. But he knows some things are more important than baseball. Albert and his wife, Deidre, started the Pujols Family Foundation in 2005. The foundation helps those affected by Down syndrome in the United States and improves the lives of thousands of impoverished people in the Dominican Republic. (Visit www.pujolsfamilyfoundation.org to find out more about Albert's ministry.) You see, Albert isn't content hitting home runs only on the field. He knows God has a plan to use his platform for a greater purpose.

You can hit a home run this Christmas by using the platform God has given you as a platform for giving. We all have a sphere of influence. Sure, most of us won't have the eyes of the whole world on us, but our family is watching. Friends at school are watching. Coworkers are watching. Make sure that this Christmas they see someone determined to give big. I'm giving you a hundred ideas on how to do it! Knock one out of the park just like Albert.

> *Bring all the tithes into the storehouse. . . . I will pour out a blessing so*
> *great you won't have enough room to take it in!*
> MALACHI 3:10

6

Say Merry Christmas to a complete stranger.

DON'T SAVE YOUR CHRISTMAS CHEER FOR FRIENDS AND FAMILY ONLY.

The Holy Spirit produces this kind of fruit in our lives: joy.

GALATIANS 5:22

Forgive before they ask for it.

This is a hard one. Who am I kidding? This may have been the hardest one for me to write down with a clear conscience. Every one of these 101 ways have forced me to take a good hard look at the reality of whether or not I could actually carry out the task, let alone ask any of you to do it. But this one is a real toughie.

There's something that happens inside of us when we feel like we're the victims of some sort of injustice. I have this ability to write people off if I feel like they have done me wrong. Can you relate? Is there someone who has done something to hurt you? Maybe the holidays bring back bitter memories of a family member who deserted you. I know it's never easy to forgive. You may say, "Matthew, you have no idea what this person did to hurt me." You're right. I don't know. But God does. And no matter what, he calls us to forgive in the same way he forgives us. Besides, the gift we will receive in return is the gift of freedom. Bitterness is a weight that gets heavier with time. Let that weight of resentment roll off your shoulders this Christmas.

Be kind to each other, tenderhearted, forgiving one another,
just as God through Christ has forgiven you.
EPHESIANS 4:32

❋ 8 ❋
Make a joyful noise.

I love watching old episodes of *The Andy Griffith Show*. Don Knotts played my favorite character, good ole deputy Barney Fife. I remember one episode when Barney joined the Mayberry choir, claiming to be quite the accomplished singer. There was only one problem: Barney could barely hold a note. He was basically tone deaf, but he didn't let that slow him down one bit. He sang his heart out as if he were God's gift to the tenor section.

These days it seems like everyone is hoping to be the next American Idol. And while I'm thankful to be one of the few who get to make music for a living, my voice doesn't sound any sweeter to God than anybody else's.

So sing like you mean it this Christmas! Can't carry a tune? Don't be embarrassed. Who cares if the people in the row in front of you don't like your rendition of "Joy to the World"? Make a JOYful noise anyway. Others may not love to hear you sing, but God does. He takes great delight in hearing the voices of his children lifting up praise to their Father. So don't hold back. Everybody now: "JOY TO THE WORLD! THE LORD IS COME! LET EARTH RECEIVE HER KING!"

Shout to the LORD, all the earth; break out in praise and sing for joy! . . .
Make a joyful symphony before the LORD, the King!
PSALM 98:4, 6

❄ **9** ❄

Be an angel of the night.

Growing up in the suburbs of Chicago, Illinois, there was never any shortage of snow in December . . . or January . . . or February. (Catch my drift?) We had crazy amounts of snow, and you know what that means—someone had to shovel the driveway. Every time we'd get hit by a snowstorm, Dad would say, "This looks like a job for the angels of the night." My brothers and I would grumble a little as we reluctantly put on our hats, gloves, and snow boots and headed out for a long night of shoveling.

We weren't shoveling our own driveway. Dad would take us to the home of a widow in our church or to the neighborhood of an elderly man who was too frail for manual labor. We worked hard, but it didn't feel like work because, despite our initial grumbling, we always had fun together. And we knew how surprised the people would be the next morning when they looked out their windows. The angels of the night had struck again.

Do you know someone who needs a job done? Someone who can't take care of it him- or herself? Be an angel of the night, and surprise someone with a secret good deed.

Be an example . . . by doing good works of every kind.
TITUS 2:7

❊ 10 ❊
Give someone a hug.

My friend Taylor has a gift. And it's a gift she loves to give. She gives just about the best hugs east of the Mississippi. They can make a grown man cry—literally.

Taylor's mother told me one such story. As the family was about to enter a restaurant one day, Taylor's eyes landed on a homeless man outside, sitting alone with a paper cup in his hand. Her parents could smell the stench of alcohol and the man's body odor as they walked past him. But Taylor wasn't put off. She kept extending her arms out to the homeless man until Taylor's mom turned to him and reluctantly said, "My daughter thinks you need a hug." The man reached out and accepted one of those famous Taylor hugs. As they embraced, tears streamed down the man's face. All because of Taylor's spontaneous act of affection.

Taylor sees the world with different eyes. This young girl with Down syndrome saw right through the dirty outward appearance of this man and into a heart that hadn't been shown love in a long time. What if we could look at people this Christmas the same way Taylor does? Something tells me we'd give a lot more hugs.

People judge by outward appearance,
but the Lord looks at the heart.
1 SAMUEL 16:7

✳ 11 ✳

Give your good stuff to Goodwill.

DONATE ITEMS WITH THE TAGS STILL ON THEM.

The generous will prosper.
PROVERBS 11:25

12

Set an extra plate at the dinner table.

Growing up, I rarely experienced a Christmas dinner with only my immediate family members. Without fail, my dad would find out about someone who didn't have anywhere to go for the holidays. A college student who couldn't afford a flight home. A single lady from the church with no family nearby. A teenager who was neglected by his parents. There was always an extra place at the table for someone outside our family to join us.

If you are blessed to be among family and friends this Christmas and you know someone who may be spending the holiday alone, invite that person to dinner. I still have friends from childhood who call my parents "Mom and Dad" because of the kindness they were shown at times like Christmas. This season, let your family be the family someone else has never had. "Home is where the heart is," as they say, and every heart should be able to call some place home at Christmas.

Get into the habit of inviting guests home for dinner.
ROMANS 12:13 (TLB)

✲ **13** ✲

Help those who help others.

I would never forgive myself if I wrote a Christmas book without at least one reference to my all-time favorite Christmas movie! I promise this is the only time I'll talk about *It's a Wonderful Life*. The film is on continuous play at my house. I just love Jimmy Stewart's character, George Bailey. Here's a guy who spends the prime of his life putting aside his own dreams to help others achieve theirs. Until one Christmas Eve, when George finds himself in a world of trouble after his uncle Billy misplaces thousands of dollars needed to keep the business afloat. George finds out how truly blessed he is when all of the people whom he helped come to his aid. Tissue, please.

Do you know someone with a thankless job? someone who is always going out of his or her way to help others? Where do those people go when they need help? They may not even ask for help when they need it, because that's just how selfless they are. Maybe there's a pastor or counselor who has walked with you through tough times this year. Maybe one of your children's teachers has given extra time and attention to help your child grow. Take the opportunity to lift up someone who lifts up so many others.

Help her in whatever she needs, for she has been helpful
to many, and especially to me.
ROMANS 16:2

❄ **14** ❄
Finish what you started.

Guys, is there a project around your house that you promised your wife you would complete? Perhaps she has been asking and asking and asking you to fix the leak in the kitchen sink, or maybe that bedroom is still waiting to be painted. Ladies, what about that mound of clothes you've been meaning to sort through to give to a secondhand shop? Well, this Christmas you could give the gift of finishing. Loose ends are not healthy. They begin to pile up until you don't even know where to start, let alone how to finish. At any given time, I seem to have plenty of loose ends out there. I can start a project like a pro, with the best of intentions to complete it.

It's one thing to be a strong starter, but what good is that if you can't finish the job? An author can't release a book of empty pages and say, "Oh yeah, I meant to finish that but never got around to it." So finish something this Christmas that you have already started. Check it off your list of loose ends. You'll feel much lighter—trust me.

Here is my advice: It would be good for you to finish what you started
a year ago. Last year you were the first who wanted to give, and you were
the first to begin doing it. Now you should finish what you started.
Let the eagerness you showed in the beginning
be matched now by your giving.
2 CORINTHIANS 8:10-11

❄ **15** ❄
Here's a tip.

Leave an enormous tip for your server after a meal in a restaurant. Who knows what kind of day that person has had? That little gesture might make a big difference in his or her day. In fact, I'll take this one a bit further. Say you happen to sit down in a restaurant this Christmas and it is obvious your server has had it. Maybe the service is so poor that you find yourself tempted to skip the gratuity completely. Well, in that case, give more! And don't worry about the extra tip validating the server's rudeness. That's not up to you. You never know what someone may be going through. People are hurting all around you this Christmas, and this is just another small way you can make a big impact.

Remember, God doesn't give grace only to those who deserve it. If that were the case, none of us would receive it. We are called to give because Christ first gave to us. Leaving a big tip this Christmas is just another way to give. And even if the service you received wasn't the best, you can leave that restaurant feeling pretty confident that the next table that server waits on will be greeted with a smile.

Everything we have has come from you,
and we give you only what you first gave us!
1 CHRONICLES 29:14

✻ 16 ✻

Pray for our soldiers on active duty

AND THOSE WHOSE FAMILIES ARE SPENDING CHRISTMAS WITHOUT THEM.

Devote yourselves to prayer with . . . a thankful heart.

COLOSSIANS 4:2

Listen—really listen.

I'm guilty. Guilty of hearing, but not listening. Just ask my wife. I must confess there have been times when I have pretended to listen to something Emily is saying to me, while watching over her shoulder to see the latest news on ESPN. What a guy thing to do, right? I know—it's pathetic. I really do have to work at being a good listener. And not just with my wife. It's difficult to focus on what someone is saying to you and really listen intently without being distracted.

Have you ever been talking to someone and the whole time you can tell that person is distracted or not really paying attention? Not a good feeling, is it? On the flip side, I know how good it feels to be heard. To know that someone is really tuned in to what I am saying, and to be confident that my words matter to them. The gift of listening may be on the Christmas wish list of someone you know. Give that gift to him or her. Make direct eye contact, really focus, and let the other person know you are listening intently to what he or she has to say.

You must all be quick to listen.

JAMES 1:19

❄ **18** ❄

Give the shirt off your back.

The phrase "give the shirt off your back" is usually just an expression. But I know a guy who actually did it! My parents were newlyweds living in Wisconsin. They did their laundry at a local Laundromat. While my dad was waiting for the clothes to dry one day, a homeless man walked in. He was shirtless, and the manager told him to leave. A few minutes later, out walked my dad with no shirt on! My mother, who was waiting for him in the parking lot, couldn't believe her eyes. When she asked him what happened, Dad said, "He needed a clean shirt, so I just gave him mine." This is love, my friends.

Chances are that most of us won't find ourselves in a situation quite like that very often. But ask yourself: "Would I be willing to actually give the shirt off my back to a stranger in need?" A true spirit of giving is found in a heart that resolves to say whatever, wherever, whenever, however.

Be rich in good works and generous to those in need,
always being ready to share with others.
1 TIMOTHY 6:18

❄ **19** ❄
Smile.

I've got lines. More wrinkles than I had when I was younger. I've noticed a few creases located right above my nose, between my eyebrows. You know the lines I'm talking about. They are the ones you get when you make that face. What face? You know—that face. The frustrated face. The worried face. The "I'm mad at the world" face. The face that says, nine out of ten things are going right, but I'm bound to be upset about the one thing going wrong. Those lines remind us of the toll that worry can take on us.

This Christmas, create new lines on your face. Lines that come from a lifetime of smiles. Mark Twain said, "Wrinkles should merely indicate where smiles have been." In a society obsessed with preserving our youth, those are wrinkles that anybody should be proud to have. "Every time you smile at someone," said Mother Teresa, "it is an action of love, a gift to that person, a beautiful thing." Giving someone a smile doesn't cost you a penny, but it can make someone else feel like a million bucks. Say cheese. . . .

A cheerful look brings joy to the heart.
PROVERBS 15:30

Keep a secret.

The Bible provides not only instructions about the importance of giving, but also the how-tos of giving. The way we go about giving matters. I recently wrote the song "Give This Christmas Away" that inspired me to write this book. The song was originally written for the VeggieTales movie *Saint Nicholas - A Story of Joyful Giving*. The movie tells the real-life story of St. Nicholas, focusing on the importance of not only giving, but giving in secret. This is how the legend of St. Nicholas was born. He would secretly help those in need. Giving isn't really giving if you're only hoping to receive the credit or praise. And God sees your heart's true motives at Christmas or, for that matter, any other time of the year.

Keep a secret this Christmas. Let your giving be a secret between you and God. Go out of your way to make sure the beneficiary of your kindness doesn't know who to thank for the blessing. You don't need to wear a red hat and grow a long, white beard, either. That gig is already covered.

*When you give to someone, don't tell your left hand what your right hand
is doing. Give your gifts in secret, and your Father,
who knows all secrets, will reward you.*
MATTHEW 6:3-4

❄ **21** ❄

Comfort the brokenhearted.

Do you know someone who is dealing with grief this Christmas? Maybe a friend has recently lost a loved one, or a young couple is dealing with a miscarriage. Pray for God to give you a greater sensitivity toward the needs and the heartbreaks of those around you this Christmas. Then ask him to open a door for you to somehow share in their sorrow and offer them comfort. It takes great discernment to be a true support for someone who is facing deep discouragement, much more than offering clichéd sentiments.

Many people suffer from seasonal depression at Christmastime. It's hard to fathom how a season filled with such joy for one person can equate to such sadness for another. For some, Christmas is just another reminder of a marriage that ended or a job that was lost. Loneliness can be a cloud that hides a broken heart during the holidays. So break through someone's loneliness this season. Accompany that friend who is ill to the next doctor's appointment. Visit the mother whose husband walked out. Cry with the brokenhearted. Let them know they are not alone this Christmas. They will find comfort in knowing that they don't have to face this season on their own.

He has sent me to comfort the brokenhearted.
ISAIAH 61:1

✻ 22 ✻

Give your best Elvis impersonation.

Many seniors spend the holidays alone in assisted living facilities. Some have families who are too busy to pay a visit, even at Christmas. When I was growing up, my family always visited a local senior citizens home during Christmas. My dad is a preacher, and every year he scheduled a special service. He made sure the whole family came along, and assured us that just our presence there would make a huge difference.

Each member of the family was involved. I sang a Christmas carol or two. My brother Joel would play his saxophone. And my youngest brother, Adam, would do his best Elvis impersonation. How funny is that! The people would applaud. They loved giving us candy, and my cheeks were sore from all the pinches the ladies gave me. We had a wonderful time. See, it didn't matter what we did while we were there. What mattered was the simple fact that we took the time to be with them. Spend time with the elderly, and encourage your children to respect their elders. Listen to the stories of Christmas past that they're eager to share. You will leave a richer person than when you arrived.

> *For the LORD your God is living among you. . . .*
> *He will rejoice over you with joyful songs.*
> ZEPHANIAH 3:17

✳ 23 ✳

Get to know a new neighbor

OR AN OLD ONE YOU'VE BEEN AVOIDING.

The Holy Spirit produces this kind of fruit in our lives: peace.
GALATIANS 5:22

❄ **24** ❄
It's payback time.

Pay back an outstanding debt that you may have with someone. The longer you go without paying somebody back, the greater the chance for resentment to build up between the two of you. This Christmas, have one less thing weighing on your conscience. Even if you can't afford to pay that person the whole amount right now, make some type of down payment to let him or her know you intend to repay the amount in full. Chances are, the person you repay could use the extra money this time of year, and it will be a welcome surprise.

Maybe someone gave you a gift or helped you out during a time when you were in need. Surprise the giver by repaying the favor, even if he or she told you it was a gift. This is a way to remember those who have helped you along the way and bless them in return.

Give to everyone what you owe them.
ROMANS 13:7

Buy a cup of coffee for a stranger.

I heard the story of someone in my church who was sitting in the Starbucks drive-through when she thought, *What would happen if I not only paid for my own coffee, but also paid for the car behind me?* The closer she got to the drive-through window, the more she smiled. *This will be fun!* So after getting her own order, she handed the cashier extra money and said, "Please tell the person in the next car that their drink has been paid for."

What happened next is pretty amazing. That next driver pulled up to pay, was momentarily confused, then was absolutely delighted to learn of the gift of free coffee. So that person decided to pay for the next customer's coffee!

Why not? They were passing on the blessing that someone had given to them. The idea spread like wildfire in the drive-through line that day. I'm told the same thing happened over fifty times! And to think, it all started with one person in one car who had one little idea. Give it a try this Christmas. Who knows? Maybe the best cup of coffee you ever buy is the one you buy for someone else.

You share with me the special favor of God.
PHILIPPIANS 1:7

Give yourself the gift of silence.

I learned this lesson the hard way. You see, a couple of years ago I was given the gift of silence, but it wasn't by choice. It seemed like the furthest thing from a gift at the time. My voice was taken away from me when I received the news from doctors that my vocal cords required surgery. For several weeks I was forced to be completely silent. No talking. No singing. Not even a whisper. My only means of communication was writing on a dry-erase board (and my handwriting rivals the messiness of my doctor's).

This "gift" was a tough pill to swallow. For the first time in a long time, I lost my ability to fill up space with words. I spent many days in solitude, and looking back, those were some of the most cherished times I've ever experienced with the Lord. The door was closed behind me. The noise of the world was shut out. And there it was—that seldom heard but precious sound—silence. Plan a time for silence each day during this Christmas season. Maybe you'll have a houseful of guests staying with you. Well, try to get up before Aunt Betty does, and spend a few moments being still and silent before the Lord. He will give you a peace that will carry you through the Christmas chaos.

Be still, and know that I am God!
PSALM 46:10

❄ 27 ❄

Read the Christmas story.

It sounds like a no-brainer, but have you ever let an entire Christmas season pass by without opening your Bible and reading the actual story of the birth of Christ? Humbly, I have to answer yes. Sure, you hear the story in church, and the kids sing about it during the special pageant. But there's something significant about taking time to read the account from Matthew or Luke's Gospel. Whether you're by yourself or with your family on Christmas, reading the story aloud will help you not to miss the reason for celebrating this season.

This is one tradition my father began that I have continued with my own family. As a kid, I'd be sitting in front of the Christmas tree, ready to tear into every present that had my name on it. But without fail, Dad would stop me, hold up the Bible, and say, "Whose turn is it to read this year?" What a fitting time to read the story! Right before we'd indulge in all of the gifts. It never failed to put things into perspective. Try adding this tradition to your Christmas morning. Take turns reading the story each year. It's a powerful thing to read about the gift that God gave us. Kind of makes that pair of Air Jordans that I thought I really wanted not that important after all.

I bring you good news that will bring great joy to all people.
The Savior—yes, the Messiah, the Lord—has been born today
in Bethlehem, the city of David!
LUKE 2:10-11

❄ 28 ❄
Cross "enemy" lines.

Don't be afraid to come to the aid of someone who is different from you this Christmas. So what if you're a Republican and that guy has an Obama bumper sticker on his car. Pull over and help him fix his flat. Be willing to help someone regardless of race, gender, religion, or lifestyle. I'll take it one step further. Go out of your way to find someone whom you might ordinarily steer clear of because of that person's different beliefs.

Jesus set the bar for all of us when it comes to reaching out to our enemies. He used the powerful parable of the Good Samaritan to teach his disciples. A Jewish man was attacked and left for dead on the side of the road. A priest passed him by, refusing to help. A Temple assistant did the same. Check out what happened next: "Then a despised Samaritan came along, and when he saw the man, he felt compassion for him" (Luke 10:33). The Samaritan crossed over enemy lines and came to the aid of this enemy in need. Jesus closed the teaching of his parable the same way I'll close this story. He said, "Now go and do the same" (Luke 10:37).

Love your neighbor as yourself.
JAMES 2:8

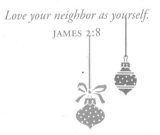

Don't let your head get in the way of your heart.

I have a confession to make. There have been times I've been approached by a homeless person on the street asking for a handout and thought to myself, *He or she is probably just going to use the money to buy alcohol or drugs instead of food or a place to stay.* Then I'd shake my head and walk away. That fear of enabling someone to continue destructive habits is often enough to keep me from giving.

Have you ever thought the same thing? Don't let your head be the judge of who is or isn't worthy of a gift. You never know. Your gift might be the one that turns a life around. Don't miss out on that opportunity. If your heart is telling you to give, that spirit of compassion is God at work in you. And if you don't feel comfortable just handing money to a stranger, ask if you can buy that person a meal or pay for the person's bus fare. God will honor your willingness to give.

> *Then these righteous ones will reply, "Lord, when did we ever see you hungry and feed you? Or thirsty and give you something to drink? Or a stranger and show you hospitality? Or naked and give you clothing? When did we ever see you sick or in prison and visit you?" And the King will say, "I tell you the truth, when you did it to one of the least of these my brothers and sisters, you were doing it to me!"*
>
> MATTHEW 25:37-40

30

Dig between the couch cushions.

COLLECT LOOSE CHANGE AROUND THE HOUSE FOR THE SALVATION ARMY KETTLE.

When God's people are in need, be ready to help them.

ROMANS 12:13

✳ **31** ✳
Care for the sick.

I remember when I first learned about HIV as a kid. There was a man in our church who became very sick and was hospitalized. He was dying of AIDS. His family was going through such heartache and needed my dad's pastoral care and support. This happened in the early nineties, when many of the facts about how AIDS can be contracted were not as commonly known as they are today. As a kid, I was afraid for my dad every time he went to visit this man. My father, on the other hand, never thought twice about going to the hospital. He regularly spent time with this man, holding his hand, praying for him and his family, and reading the Bible with him. When the man died, my father preached at his funeral. There, Dad had the opportunity to share the message of hope in Christ with people who ordinarily wouldn't find themselves in a church.

Jesus used the word *sick* as a metaphor for a lost and dying world. So whether you are caring for someone with a physical sickness or someone with a spiritual sickness, this kind of giving takes deeper faith. It is a willingness to go below the surface, to really dig in and say, "Okay, God, I will go where you want me to go—anywhere."

Healthy people don't need a doctor—sick people do.
MATTHEW 9:12

❄ **32** ❄
Pass the buck.

Take some five-, ten-, and twenty-dollar bills, and spend an afternoon with your family finding places to put the bills where someone who needs them will find them. This could be a fun activity for everyone, sort of a reverse scavenger hunt. It's another way to give in secret. While you are running around hiding the money, imagine the story a single mother might tell about how she could barely afford groceries and then she found a twenty taped to her grocery cart. Try to picture the look on the face of a homeless person who finds the money on the ground next to the Dumpster.

Alexander Pope wrote, "Do good by stealth, and blush to find it fame." Use this experience of "stealth" giving to discuss with your coconspirators why giving doesn't need to come with any recognition or credit. God sees what is done in secret and that's all that matters.

When we take your gifts to those who need them, they will thank God.
2 CORINTHIANS 9:11

❄ **33** ❄

Volunteer at a
homeless shelter <u>after</u> Christmas.

The truth is, homeless shelters, food banks, and other places like them probably wish they had as much volunteer help the rest of the year as they do during the holidays. So while you are in the spirit of the Christmas season, arrange another day in the future to serve. But here's the challenge: stick to it. Mark the date down in your calendar, and no matter how busy your schedule becomes in January or beyond, make that promise to work at the shelter a commitment that you refuse to break.

If you give even a cup of cold water
to one of the least of my followers,
you will surely be rewarded.

MATTHEW 10:42

❄ **34** ❄

Be patient with your (annoying) relatives.

Everybody's got 'em. I'm sure if I asked you, you could quickly rattle off the name of a relative who tends to outstay his or her welcome over the holidays. The movie *Elf* nails one of the classic depictions of dysfunctional family visits during the holidays. The main character, Buddy, was raised as an elf at the North Pole—a six-foot-tall elf dressed in green with bright yellow tights. He is searching for his real family in New York City, and when he finds them, well, let's just say that the family isn't quite as thrilled as he is. Buddy makes them spaghetti with maple syrup for breakfast, uses the wood from an armoire to build a rocking horse, and gets thrown in jail after announcing that a department-store Santa is a fake. Buddy has nothing but love for his new family, and he means well. So do your relatives.

Go out of your way to show love to a particular relative whom you have a hard time getting along with. Chances are, they will respond in a positive way. And pray for an extra dose of patience when dealing with your family this Christmas. Just hope they don't show up at your house in yellow tights.

Be patient with each other, making allowance for
each other's faults because of your love.
EPHESIANS 4:2

Collect a cart.

TAKE YOUR GROCERY CART BACK AND GRAB SOMEONE ELSE'S TOO.

Serve each other in humility.

I PETER 5:5

Give till it hurts.

Give dangerously this Christmas. To give cautiously is to show more concern for your own well-being than for someone else's need. True giving should require some sort of sacrifice. If the gift you are giving to your church or an organization doesn't hurt the wallet a bit, give it a second thought. Is there something you could go without that might cause some inconvenience but allow you to give more?

   I like the wonderful challenge that Mother Teresa presents to us. "Give! Give the love we have all received to those around you. Give until it hurts, because real love hurts. That is why you must love until it hurts."

Jesus told him, "If you want to be perfect, go and sell all your possessions and give the money to the poor, and you will have treasure in heaven. Then come, follow me." But when the young man heard this, he went away sad, for he had many possessions. Then Jesus said to his disciples, "I tell you the truth, it is very hard for a rich person to enter the Kingdom of Heaven."
MATTHEW 19:21-23

❄ **37** ❄

Take the first step.

It's easy to give gifts at Christmas to the ones you love, isn't it? I would imagine that the people who are on your Christmas shopping list are people whom you are quite fond of. How about enemies? Got any of those on your list this Christmas? Most people aren't racing to the stores to buy a gift for that special archnemesis in their lives. Does someone come to mind who would be completely shocked to receive a gift or a card from you this Christmas?

Well, what if you did it? What if you shocked that enemy of yours by taking the first step? (If you are still a little uncertain, please see no. 7 for reinforcement on the importance of forgiveness.) Even if it seems like it's too big a step to actually give gifts to our enemies, we are still called to pray for them. That is something we can all stand to be reminded of. I know that's not my first instinct when I think of someone who has hurt me. Love your enemies. We learned the lesson in Sunday school. Consider this a little refresher course.

You have heard the law that says, "Love your neighbor" and hate your enemy. But I say, love your enemies! Pray for those who persecute you! In that way, you will be acting as true children of your Father in heaven.

MATTHEW 5:43-45

❄ **38** ❄
Be a clean freak.

When Grandfather West was alive, he was always on self-appointed trash duty. Everywhere he went, he always took the time to stop and pick up trash he saw lying around. He passed this trait on to my dad. If Dad notices an empty soda can on the sidewalk or a crumpled-up newspaper in someone's yard, he takes the time to pick it up and throw it away. I used to roll my eyes when Dad did that, thinking he was crazy. But now I realize the real root of this act. He takes the trash he finds to a receptacle because if he doesn't do it, someone else will have to. What a powerful principle to live by! Instead of assuming somebody else will do a job that needs to be done, Grandpa and Dad took it upon themselves to collect trash that wasn't even theirs.

These types of acts can only come from a person with a servant's heart. The higher a person thinks of him- or herself, the less likely he or she will be to serve others. Imagine if all of us lived with one motivation: to serve. The impact would be felt throughout our neighborhoods, our churches, our communities, and our world. If you want to be great in God's Kingdom, pick up a little trash this Christmas.

Whoever wants to be a leader among you must be your servant.
MATTHEW 20:26

❄ **39** ❄
Explore the world.

As a family, find a country in need outside of the United States. Commit to supporting that particular area of the world financially instead of spending money on a typical Christmas. What an awesome way to teach your children about other parts of the world and the hardships people face every day! You can work through reliable relief organizations that are in the business of providing food, medicine, and clean water to some of the most impoverished corners of the world.

So get out a map, do some Web browsing, and learn about another culture. With some organizations, you can even follow the progress of current work projects in villages. This exercise will create a new appreciation for the luxuries we enjoy every day in the United States. At the same time, learning about another part of the world in need will stir a greater sensitivity for the pain and suffering that we seldom bother thinking about. Go to www.givethischristmasaway.com for more information about relief organizations.

Go into all the world and preach the Good News to everyone.
MARK 16:15

Use your hands.

Instead of buying a Christmas gift, make someone a gift this year. Perhaps you have a special skill or hobby that you could put to use in creating a more meaningful gift than just another sweater from the store. My friend Kimmy is the daughter of my high school baseball coach, and she's one of the most thoughtful people you'll meet. She makes blankets. Fluffy, perfect fleece blankets. I don't know how she does it exactly. It's just something she does well. She sent a blanket for both of my daughters when they were born, and another for our dog, Earl (even though Earl thinks every blanket in the house is hers).

Every year my favorite gifts are the ones that I can tell someone put a lot of thought into. If it means something to you, it will mean something to the recipient. So don't be afraid to give your hands more of a workout this Christmas. Put your heart into it, and just like Kimmy's blankets are to our family, your gift will be one to remember and cherish.

Commit your actions to the LORD, and your plans will succeed.
PROVERBS 16:3

❄ 41 ❄

Give a memory.

Instead of filling your house with material possessions this Christmas, you and your family could give each other a memory. Take the money you would spend on Christmas presents and put it toward a special family getaway. Growing up, some of my fondest memories were family vacations. My parents never had much money, but they would save and save every year in the hopes of taking the whole family on a trip. In the summer, my brothers and I would pile in the back of our red Ford station wagon with its hot vinyl seats that our legs always stuck to, and off we'd go to make a memory.

Recently I was talking about finances with my father. He is nearing retirement, and when I asked him what his savings situation was like, his answer surprised me. "Son, you see all those photo albums from our family vacations? Those are my savings account." You're right, Dad, and I believe your investment has paid off. Those wonderful family memories are priceless in my book. This Christmas invest in something that matters. Give each other a memory your family will not soon forget.

Those who are wise will take all this to heart; they will see in our history the faithful love of the LORD.

PSALM 107:43

* 42 *

Hug a grinch
this Christmas.

YOU JUST MIGHT MELT AN ICY HEART.

The Holy Spirit produces this kind of fruit in our lives: love.

GALATIANS 5:22

❄ **43** ❄

Invite a friend to church.

The holidays are a time when many people who would normally never darken the door of a church may be more open than usual to hearing the message of hope in Christ. Churches everywhere hold special services and Christmas programs in hopes of reaching their communities beyond their own members. The problem is, so many Christians can get caught up in an exclusive mind-set about their church life. I know I can develop this sort of compartmentalized approach to my faith. Before I know it, I've created a church world and a secular world. And I am reluctant for the two to ever meet.

Think about it. Do you have any unsaved friends? When was the last time you invited a friend to church? Step out of your comfort zone at Christmas. Find out what special events might be happening at your church that you would feel comfortable inviting a non-Christian friend to. Share your faith this Christmas. We have been given the precious gift of God's love. We must not keep that gift all to ourselves.

*Let your light shine for all to see. For the glory of the L*ORD
rises to shine on you.
ISAIAH 60:1

❄ **44** ❄
Leave a message.

Sing a Christmas song on someone's answering machine. Sing it loud; it doesn't matter if it's off key. My family members still call each other and sing "Happy Birthday" to the celebrant. It's always a voice mail I don't want to delete. So pretend you're auditioning for *American Idol*, warm up the pipes, and sing your heart out until the machine cuts you off.

You'll bring a smile to someone's face and have a fun time too. It's a little thing, leaving a silly message to let someone know they are being thought of at Christmas. But for some, that will be a welcome reminder.

Every time I think of you, I give thanks to my God.
PHILIPPIANS 1:3

❄ **45** ❄

Do it again.

Pick one of the ways to give this Christmas away that you've read and that you have already done . . . and do it again. Make sure your attitude toward giving is beyond just checking these good deeds off as you do them. The goal is not to create some sort of giving to-do list. It's about waking up the giving spirit in all of us and committing ourselves to a new way of looking at the world. William Penn possessed that kind of spirit: "I expect to pass through life but once. If therefore, there be any kindness I can show, or any good thing I can do to any fellow being, let me do it now, and not defer or neglect it, as I shall not pass this way again."

Is there one particular way to give that you have already completed, but you felt especially enthusiastic in the midst of doing it and invigorated when you were done? These 101 ways are not mere suggestions or just feel-good thoughts. My hope is that you might walk away from this little giving manual with a new attitude of generosity for you to take into your everyday life, even after Christmas is over.

> *What good is it . . . if you say you have faith*
> *but don't show it by your actions?*
>
> JAMES 2:14

46

Take it to the bank.

Start a savings account specifically for the purpose of giving. Then raise money to put in the savings account every month. Make a goal of how much money you want to save for the year. When Christmas rolls around next year, pray and decide how you will give all of the money away. Then start saving for next year!

We put aside money for lots of different things. We save up for that vacation and invest in our retirement funds. We put money in the stock market and make sure we can pay our monthly mortgages. So why not be just as deliberate with our giving? This is something you can do by yourself, with a spouse, or with the entire family. Each month's statement will reveal how every penny adds up. Your children will see your heart for giving and will remember this when they have children. I just love the thought of saving money for the sole purpose of giving it away. A project like this says, "I take my giving seriously." Besides, the money you save will earn interest over a year's time, allowing you to give even more.

God has given gifts to each of you. . . . Manage them well so
that God's generosity can flow through you.
1 PETER 4:10

✳ **47** ✳

Make
a coupon.

**KIDS, WRITE OUT "WORK" COUPONS
TO GIVE TO YOUR PARENTS—THEY'RE
INEXPENSIVE AND THOUGHTFUL.**

*A good person produces good things from
the treasury of a good heart.*

LUKE 6:45

Read a book to a child . . . and then read it "one more time."

My daughter Lulu absolutely loves when I sit and read books to her. Most nights I am convinced her love of reading is influenced by her desire to stay up past her bedtime. It's amazing how many times you can read the same story over and over again. I'll come to the end of the last page, and she'll look at me with eyes that could melt an iceberg and say, "Can you please read it one more time, Daddy? Just one more time?" Even if this is a three-year-old's premeditated master plan to squeeze a few extra minutes before bed, the fact is, she wants to spend time with her daddy. How can I say no to that?

So here's the deal. I'm not going to recommend that you do away completely with your normal lights out schedule. I'm simply saying that when your school-age children are home for Christmas break, they want to spend time with you. Could it really hurt to read a favorite book again? Or how about reading to a young family member you visit at Christmastime? Pretty soon, that little girl or boy won't be so little, and we'll wish we would have read that same book about a million times more. Time to move on. I'm getting a little emotional. . . .

Children are a gift from the LORD.
PSALM 127:3

Give yourself a silent night.

Turn all the cell phones off. Turn off your television and hide the remote control. For one night, resist video games, computers, and CDs. Try your best to create a silent night. You can even turn the lights off and light some candles around your house. We live in such a loud world. Media dominates our lives. According to the Nielsen Company, the average American watches more than four hours of TV each day! Daily distractions can prevent us from experiencing a moment of peace. The Christmas season can be the worst of all, sending us into sensory overload.

By choosing a silent night, you are giving yourself the chance to experience peace away from the noise this Christmas. In the stillness of your silent night, try to imagine a starry night near Bethlehem where an angel of the Lord appeared, bringing the shepherds the good news of Jesus' birth. What if those shepherds had been carrying on and were too distracted to notice the angel? I think many times the question is not, Is God speaking? but rather, Am I listening? Clear away the distractions tonight and answer that question with a resounding yes.

The shepherds went back to their flocks, glorifying and praising
God for all they had heard and seen.

LUKE 2:20

Have an advent-ure.

Instead of the traditional Advent calendar that features activities or treats, pick out a different person to pray for every day leading up to Christmas (December 1 to December 24). You can do this as a family. Parents, make sure your children help select the people your family will pray for. Don't discourage any of their ideas. No name is off limits. You can also do this by yourself, making a list of people that God puts on your heart. You can dedicate one whole day to praying for a missionary family that you or your church supports. You can spend one day praying for our president. Pray for friends, enemies, even celebrities. Heavens, pray for me! Lord knows, I need it.

On many occasions, I've had people I've never met before come up and tell me they were praying for me. I can't tell you how good it feels to discover that somewhere out there, someone was storming the gates of heaven on *my* behalf. Knowing that you are prayed for—there is no greater gift.

Never stop praying.
I THESSALONIANS 5:17

Cross the big one off your list.

Take a look at your Christmas wish list. What's the most expensive item? How much do you really need it? Is the item something you could live without? I'm asking you to be 100 percent honest here. Is this item on your wish list A) a luxury or B) a necessity? If you answered A, then take a deep breath and cross it off your list.

If you are really serious about giving this Christmas away, it's not possible without some sacrifice. This is just another way to make a conscious effort to think about someone other than yourself this year. After you cross that item off of your list, you can estimate the approximate dollar amount of the gift you wanted. Then, instead of asking someone to buy you the gift, request that he or she make a charitable donation for that same amount. The gift giver can even make that donation in your name. This one might sting a bit, but it's a good thing. Trust me.

Don't store up treasures here on earth, where moths eat them
and rust destroys them, and where thieves break in and steal.
Store your treasures in heaven, where moths and rust cannot destroy,
and thieves do not break in and steal.
MATTHEW 6:19-20

52

Bake an extra dozen.

There's nothing like the smell of fresh cookies baking in the oven. You're wrapping presents by the fireplace, watching your favorite Christmas movie (You all know what mine is, right? See no. 13.), and then all of a sudden that sweet, sweet cookie aroma winds its way in your direction. I'm actually a big fan of cookie dough as well. Anybody else with me on that one? When my wife bakes cookies, I always make her set aside some dough for me to enjoy. Sorry—I'm digressing.

This year, double the recipe. Make more and give more. Don't just make that batch of sugar cookies for your family party. Bake an extra dozen and drop them off at your friend's house or the house of the new family on the block. This gift has a unique personal touch. All of you bakers, maybe you have a special recipe that you want to tape to the top of the box of cookies. Who knows, your new neighbor might return the favor, and you know what that means—more cookies for you. Is anybody else hungry?

Make the most of every opportunity for doing good.
EPHESIANS 5:16

Be a babysitter.

OFFER A COUPLE WITH YOUNG CHILDREN A MUCH-NEEDED NIGHT OUT.

Let's not merely say that we love each other;
let us show the truth by our actions.

1 JOHN 3:18

Say Merry Christmas outdoors.

The way to enjoy winter is to play in it if you can. Whether you live in northern climates with mounds of snow or in warmer beach locations, think of creating a Christmas gift for all to see. International artists have built elaborate nativity scenes out of sand; who's stopping you from doing it at your local beach? You can incorporate as many natural materials into your masterpiece as you can find. If you find a starfish to shine down on "Bethlehem," you get extra points in my book.

I grew up in the suburbs of Chicago, where there was never any shortage of wonderful, beautiful snow! In between sledding and snowball fights, how about building a manger scene out of snow? If you're ambitious, get your gloves on and get to work. Don't have that much energy or artistic vision? Write a message in the snow—"Glory to God and peace on earth"—for passersby to see. Or on Christmas Eve, take a moment and flap your wings in the snow or sand, remembering the angels who celebrated Jesus' arrival.

> *Suddenly, the angel was joined by a vast host of others—the armies of heaven—praising God and saying, "Glory to God in highest heaven, and peace on earth to those with whom God is pleased."*
>
> LUKE 2:13-14

❄ **55** ❄

Kick it old school.
Brown-bag it to work.

I love eating out. It started when I was single and had absolutely no desire to cook. Since then, it has become a pretty expensive way of life that I have to keep in check. So with this one, I'm definitely preaching to the choir. Instead of eating expensive meals at restaurants all the time, bring your lunch to work. Don't worry; Chili's will still be there in January. But for December, take the extra money you save by making your own PB and J, and give it to someone else.

There are so many small sacrifices we can make, and, as we do, we will find a greater ability to give. Here's another thought: take the money you save from avoiding restaurants this month and buy groceries for a local food bank. That would be a cool way to bring your sacrifice full circle this season.

Blessed are those who are generous, because they feed the poor.
PROVERBS 22:9

Reconnect.

Look up an old friend with whom you have lost touch. Our lives get so hectic and wrapped up in our own families, jobs, and daily demands that it's hard to keep in contact with friends. On many occasions, I have thought about a friend and found myself saying, "I wonder how he or she is" or "I need to call that person." What about you? Well, do it this Christmas. Pick up the phone. My college buddies do a much better job of keeping in touch with me than I do with them. I'm pretty lousy at returning phone calls. I need to do better. Is there someone you care about but haven't spoken to lately? The next time that name pops into your head, dial the person's number right away. Don't put it off.

My friend Steve and I went to junior high and high school together. It would be easy for us to lose touch because he lives across the country, but whenever I'm in California for a show, we get together. Somehow it always feels like we are just picking up where we left off. Spend a few minutes getting reconnected to an old friend this Christmas. You won't regret it. And chances are it will feel like you never lost touch in the first place.

A friend is always loyal, and a brother is born to help in time of need.
PROVERBS 17:17

❄ **57** ❄

Beat your parents to the punch.

Kids, this one's for you. Spend an entire day making sure you obey your parents. Actually, you should spend *every* day trying to do this. But let's just take it a day at a time. The first time you are asked to do something, do it. Your parents love you very much and want what is best for you. Don't make them have to ask you over and over again to clean your room. And in some cases, maybe you can even beat them to the punch. If you see that the trash needs to be taken out or the dog hasn't had her walk yet, take care of it. The only thing better than obeying your parents when they ask you to do something is doing it before they even ask. It's a small but significant way of showing your parents that you respect and love them. In return, they will trust and respect you more.

Honor your father and mother.
Then you will live a long, full life in the land
the LORD your God is giving you.
EXODUS 20:12

❄ **58** ❄
Say cheese.

Give a special photograph to someone you love this Christmas. Put it in a really nice frame. Every year my wife schedules a secret photo shoot for herself and our two little girls and then surprises me at Christmas with a beautiful framed picture of the most important people in my life. The walls of my writing room are lined with these precious pictures capturing some of the most beautiful smiles I know. Your picture could also be as simple as a snapshot taken on a family vacation or even a picture of a loved one who has died. What a great way to help someone remember the legacy that loved one left behind.

It's the personal touch that counts when you give this Christmas. Showing someone that you put great thought and care into a gift means so much more than the amount of money you spend. We tend to get that concept backwards sometimes, thinking if we throw money at someone that might communicate our love to them. Well, all I know is, I can't remember many other things I got for Christmas last year. But I am touched by those pictures on my wall every time I look at them.

You are my friends. . . . Love each other.
JOHN 15:15, 17

❄ **59** ❄

Give your favorite Bible verses.

To say my mom is an amazing woman would be like saying the Pacific Ocean is pretty big. She is a true prayer warrior and loves the Lord with all her heart. She clings to Scripture, and I know she prays for me every single day. This Christmas idea is inspired by something she has done for years. She takes a spiral notebook of three-by-five-inch index cards and fills each card with a different Bible verse. She has always done this for herself to use during her quiet times and has also given the note cards as gifts.

I came across one of her personal notebooks one time, and as I thumbed through the Scriptures, I noticed some of the ink was blotchy. *Tear stains.* I was so moved by the thought of my mom praying and meditating over these verses that I was inspired to do the same. So I asked her to make a notebook of verses for me. Now I take these little notebooks on the road. They help me memorize Scripture. This is an inexpensive yet thoughtful gift to give someone this Christmas. It's also a good stocking stuffer. Write a little note on the first card, explaining what it is and why you chose the verses you did.

Your word is a lamp to guide my feet and a light for my path.
PSALM 119:105

60

Lose your cool.

FORGET COOL POINTS. HAVE A BLAST CAROLING DOOR-TO-DOOR WITH FRIENDS.

Sing psalms and hymns and spiritual songs to God with thankful hearts.
COLOSSIANS 3:16

❅ **61** ❅
Watch your words.

Here's a way you can give this Christmas by actually holding something back. Words are something many of us tend to throw around quite carelessly. Have you ever been unnecessarily critical of a coworker? Ever get mixed up in a little church gossip? It seems I say something regrettable to someone almost daily. I will speak out of frustration to my wife, using harsh or negative words. No sooner do those critical words leave my lips than I wish I could take them back. On the other hand, there's no greater feeling than knowing your words have just lifted someone up. Your words have the power to encourage, but they also have the power to destroy.

When it comes to your words this Christmas, think about taking a "less is more" approach. Ask God to help you filter your thoughts and show greater discernment in knowing which words are best left unsaid. Ask yourself, "Is what I want to say right now going to be life giving to this person?" If the answer is no, then hold off. This is a gift that others may not even know they've received.

Let your conversation be gracious and attractive so that you will
have the right response for everyone.
COLOSSIANS 4:6

❋ **62** ❋

Give the gift of forgetfulness.

Have you ever forgotten where you put your keys and then found them in the ignition with your car running? Or searched for your sunglasses only to find them resting on your head? If so, then this one's for you. Actually, this one is for all of us. Occasionally I have a hard time remembering things. Okay, it's pretty much all the time. I couldn't tell you what I had for breakfast. But there are certain things I remember and hold on to—like a silly morning disagreement with my wife. She can say the smallest thing that rubs me the wrong way, and I'll let it eat at me the rest of the day. By evening, that little disagreement blows up into a big argument about nothing, all because I couldn't let go of that meaningless frustration.

So, here's an inexpensive but powerful way to give this Christmas. Be forgetful. Let the little things slide. If someone offends you, don't dwell on it. I don't know about you, but I am so thankful that God is forgetful when it comes to my wrongdoings. When we ask, he forgives *and* forgets. Ask God to help you give that same gift of forgetfulness to someone this December.

He has removed our sins as far from us as the east is from the west.
PSALM 103:12

❄ 63 ❄
Get away.

My wife is reading a book called *A Woman After God's Own Heart*, and she read this passage to me that made me think of another way to give this Christmas: "You cannot be *with* people all of the time and have a ministry *to* people. The impact of your ministry to people will be in direct proportion to the time you spend away from people and with God."

I'm a people person, which is a good thing in my line of work. I perform over a hundred shows a year, and after every concert I sign autographs. One of my favorite parts of touring is meeting and talking with the people who listen to my music. But it can also be incredibly draining. I find that if I am not spending adequate time alone during the day, I am not always able to give people my full attention.

So treat yourself to a getaway. Even if it's only for a few minutes a day. Get in the Word. Ask God to give you the patience and energy to be at your best for your kids, your spouse, your parents, and the rest of the world outside your door this Christmas. He is waiting for you. Give him your time.

The LORD is my shepherd; I have all that I need. He lets me rest in green meadows; he leads me beside peaceful streams. He renews my strength.

PSALM 23:1-3

Give what they want, not what you want for them.

Do you know someone who always seems to be a bit off when it comes to picking the right Christmas gift for you? They may even ask you what you might like and then give you something completely different! Of course, you say thank you, but doesn't it feel like the thoughtfulness is cut a bit short? I call this way of giving the "buying a baseball bat for Grandma" syndrome. "What's that, Grandma? You don't play baseball? Bummer. Well, I guess I'll just have to take this off your hands!"

This type of generosity can be easily perceived as selfish. You care enough for someone that you want to give that person a gift, but you don't care enough to find out what he or she would really like. I know people who use Christmas shopping as a way to satisfy their own particular style or taste. This is a surefire way to cut the impact of a gift short. Instead, get to know someone well enough so that even if you surprise the recipient with something that wasn't on his or her list, it will be a good surprise.

P.S. I do think that everyone on your list this year would enjoy this book, though. ☺

Honesty guides good people.
PROVERBS 11:3

❄ **65** ❄
Spread the Word.

When I hear a great new CD or fall in love with a book, I am quick to tell all of my friends about it. Why don't I do that more often with the most important book ever written? The Bible has completely changed my life with God's messages of hope and instructions for living. Its pages are filled with the promise of forgiveness and the hope for eternity in heaven. Needless to say, the Bible is a MUST-READ. Yet I rarely give this treasure away to someone as a gift. What stops us from giving a gift like a Bible? Perhaps it's the fear of what others might think. These days we can become so scared of offending the world that our arms stop reaching out into it.

The shelves of your local bookstore are lined with self-help books. I am sure many of them do provide positive tools for living. But there is only one book you could give to someone this Christmas that is life giving. Tell people you care about them and want to see them in heaven someday by giving them Bibles. You can write little notes on the inside about how much this book has meant to you, along with a favorite Scripture.

All Scripture is inspired by God and is useful to teach us what is true and to make us realize what is wrong in our lives. It corrects us when we are wrong and teaches us to do what is right.
2 TIMOTHY 3:16

66

Give
some gas.

SURPRISE YOUR SPOUSE
WITH A FULL TANK OF GAS IN THE CAR.

The Holy Spirit produces this kind of fruit in our lives: goodness.

GALATIANS 5:22

Give parents a verbal ovation.

Being a parent is one of the hardest jobs in the world. But oftentimes, people are quicker with parenting critiques than passing out deserved compliments. What you say, even in loving construction, can become an emotional burr that festers in a parent's heart. I hope that each time you get together with family or friends who have children, you pat those parents on the back rather than wagging an "I told you so" in their faces. One grateful recipient explained what that looks like.

"My aunt and uncle, whom I probably haven't seen or talked with in eight years, live in Colorado. [The niece lives in Illinois.] This past summer, my parents took our two boys to visit them on vacation. During the time they were together, my aunt called me just to tell me how polite the boys were and what a good job my husband and I are doing raising our sons. I can't begin to tell you what that phone call meant to me. This past year has been a particularly tough year with one of our sons, and a number of times I've wished I'd done some things differently. Her unexpected phone call left me feeling good all weekend." Can you think of a parent whose spirit you can boost today?

Let everything you say be good and helpful, so that your words will be
an encouragement to those who hear them.
EPHESIANS 4:29

❄ **68** ❄

Give the present of being present.

I read an article in *USA Today* about people and their digital addictions. One woman confessed she sends an average of seven hundred text messages a day! She also said that once, while on vacation in Hawaii, she tried to cut down her computer time to only four hours a day. Four hours! We have come so far in creating ways to connect with each other. But somewhere between Twitter, Facebook, MySpace, e-mail, and text messages, we begin losing the ability to focus in one-on-one situations. My daughter was trying to play with me last night, but I was distracted by this book I am writing. After a few failed attempts to get my attention, she finally said, "Daddy, turn off your computer."

This Christmas, don't let yourself get so caught up in all these virtual worlds that you miss out on real life going on around you. If you meet a friend for coffee, shut your phone off so you won't be distracted. When you get home from work, leave your laptop in the car, and try to forget all the e-mails awaiting your replies. Be present with people. This gift will go a long way.

Be an example . . . in what you say, in the way you live.
1 TIMOTHY 4:12

❄ **69** ❄
Start a club.

This isn't your ordinary club. The sole purpose of this club is to find a family in need and provide a Christmas they will never forget. I remember being assigned this project in one of my high school classes. The class was split into groups and each group was assigned a family. It was our job to raise money to provide Christmas for that family. If we hadn't done our job, they would have had nothing that Christmas.

Your giving club could consist of your family, a church youth group, or a Bible study. You will experience an exhilarating feeling of unity with the people with whom you join. Lifelong friendships can be forged when people come together in the name of giving. And so much can be accomplished when we all share the responsibility.

Two people are better off than one,
for they can help each other succeed. If one person falls,
the other can reach out and help. But someone
who falls alone is in real trouble.
ECCLESIASTES 4:9-10

❄ 70 ❄

Give your sorrow away.

No one is immune to experiencing a devastating loss over the holidays, especially the death of a loved one. A story was shared with me about a single mother who lost her only daughter, Jenna, in a horrible car accident involving a drunk driver. It happened right before Thanksgiving. The mom cried out to God: "Be thankful? For what? Jenna was supposed to be home for Thanksgiving; instead, she's gone forever." All Thanksgiving Day the mom pleaded, "God, stop the pain."

As she sat crying and praying in her daughter's room, her eyes were drawn to a picture. Jenna was smiling with a large group of children she had helped on a mission trip. That instant, the mother heard her daughter's voice: "Mom, I'm okay. I'm with Jesus. Go help those who have so little and might not know Jesus." So she did, bringing the love of Jesus to little ones in a Mexican orphanage. Even though the mother still had a lot more questions for God, she was thankful that her gift to others helped keep sorrow from overtaking her heart.

If you are hurting this Christmas, think about helping someone else with the gift of your time, your talents, or your treasures.

Give your burdens to the LORD, and he will take care of you.
PSALM 55:22

Crack an egg.

Growing up, my two younger brothers and I had a little tradition every Christmas morning that my parents always seemed to appreciate. The excitement of Christmas made it impossible for us to sleep in. We would wake up before our parents, head to the kitchen, and make breakfast in bed for Mom and Dad. As you can imagine, our creation was anything but a culinary masterpiece. The eggs were usually runny, the toast charred, and the coffee was guaranteed to put hair on your chest and grounds in your teeth. Nevertheless, we tried, and my parents looked forward to their "special" breakfast every year.

Maybe you're like me, and the microwave is the only kitchen appliance you know how to work. Well, give this a try. Crack an egg or two. Find a recipe online that seems easy enough and make breakfast for someone you love. I guarantee this: even if your meal is awful, it will make for a good laugh, and the recipient will appreciate your effort! Oh, and don't leave the dishes for someone else to do. My wife taught me that lesson!

Continue to love one another, for love comes from God.
I JOHN 4:7

※ **72** ※

Give this book away.

IF THIS BOOK HAS HELPED YOU RETHINK GIVING, START A REVOLUTION.

With God's help we will do mighty things.

PSALM 60:12

❄ 73 ❄
Give a goat.

Yep, you read that correctly! This Christmas you could buy a goat. Now don't worry, you don't have to keep it in your backyard. You're not buying the goat for yourself. You can purchase a goat for a family in a foreign country who needs it to provide milk, cheese, butter, and other food. There are different relief organizations whose Christmas catalogs feature goats, chickens, and cows instead of cardigans, CD players, and remote control toys.

You and I may not realize just how valuable a goat can be. But with the help of a relief organization, your animal could literally be a life-saving gift for someone who receives it. I love this way of giving, because you or your family are able to have a specific, tangible idea of what your money is going to provide and how it will improve a person's life, family, and possibly village. Visit www.givethischristmasaway.com for resources.

O LORD, what a variety of things you have made!
In wisdom you have made them all. The earth
is full of your creatures.
PSALM 104:24

❄ **74** ❄
Be that house.

As parents, create the kind of atmosphere in your house that your children's friends will want to be around. When I was a kid, my parents always welcomed my friends over. Sometimes I wondered if my friends were coming over to my house to hang out with me or just because they loved being around my parents so much. My buddies loved hanging out with my dad. He would take us to play baseball all the time. Dad would show up at my baseball games with a cooler of sodas and give one to each of my teammates. That's the kind of dad I want to be. The truth is, some of your children's friends or the kids in your neighborhood may live in unhealthy family situations and are desperately looking for the love they don't receive at home. Some may come from an abusive home or one where parents are constantly fighting.

This Christmas, make your house the place where love is apparent as soon as someone walks in the door. Learn the names of your children's friends, and open your home to them. Not only will you be showing your own kids that you care about the important people in their lives, but you just might provide the care and support that another child needs.

God is love, and all who live in love live in God, and God lives in them.
1 JOHN 4:16

❄ 75 ❄
Pick up the tab.

I came across a story about Super Bowl champion Kurt Warner and a tradition he and his family have. Whenever they go out to eat, they choose another person or family in the restaurant and anonymously pay for the strangers' meals in addition to their own. Kurt's wife, Brenda, recalled a time when they couldn't afford to go out to dinner very often, and now that she is able to enjoy such a luxury, she says, "I look around and think there's got to be people that saved up to be able to go out to dinner or are worried about what that bill is going to be when it comes."

Imagine how good it would feel to be on the receiving end of a gift like this. It's a simple but powerful way to secretly bless someone this Christmas! This could be one of your random acts of kindness as well (see no. 25). If you have children, picking up someone else's tab is an opportunity to demonstrate to them how much God has blessed your family and how fun it is to be a secret blessing giver.

I take joy in doing your will, my God,
for your instructions are written on my heart.
PSALM 40:8

Put on a show.

This idea is inspired by my childhood, growing up as a preacher's kid. For some reason, my dad had this crazy idea every Christmas that our family should create a skit for the Sunday morning congregation. Needless to say, my brothers and I were pulled into this production kicking and screaming. Still, Dad was convinced that every member of the family had to play a part. He called it *Another West Family Christmas.* The script was strangely similar every year. The Partridges and the Osmonds had nothing to worry about. But we sang, laughed, and shared the story of Christmas. Our production never won a Tony Award, but the church members were kind enough not to boo us off the stage.

Turn your living room into a performance hall and put on your own family play this Christmas. Beforehand, write down the names of different characters from the Nativity story on pieces of paper. Have each member of the family draw a name. Then try a little improvisation and see what kind of theater masterpiece you can create. Let your children be the stars, because they're guaranteed to make you laugh. Your gift of real family entertainment will be talked about for years.

For everything there is a season, . . . a time to laugh . . .
and a time to dance.
ECCLESIASTES 3:1, 4

❄ 77 ❄

Take a day off.

GIVE YOUR FAMILY MEMBERS TIME WITH YOU DURING THE WEEK.

Love each other. Just as I have loved you,
you should love each other.

JOHN 13:34

Pay it backward.

Can you think back over the course of your life and remember someone who helped you get to where you are today? someone who mentored you? Maybe it was a coach who always brought out the best in you, or a teacher who encouraged you in your studies. It could be a person who had a direct influence on the career path you chose. My junior high choir teacher, Mrs. Severik, was one of those people in my life. At thirteen, I wasn't nearly as interested in music as I was in baseball. But she saw something in me and refused to let it go. I'll never forget the first solo she gave me. It was a song from the musical *Oklahoma*. With a little push from my teacher, I was belting out, "There's a bright golden haze on the meadow."

I can see now that God placed people like Mrs. Severik in my path to affirm the direction he had planned for me and to help birth a dream in my heart. This Christmas send a card or thank-you letter to a person who has impacted your life. Let your mentor know how he or she has helped you become the person you are today.

For I know the plans I have for you . . . plans for good . . .
to give you a future and a hope.
JEREMIAH 29:11

❄ 79 ❄

Throw a birthday party.

Friends of mine throw a birthday party every December, even though no one in the family was born that month. They throw a party honoring Jesus—the precious gift whom God sent to earth for you and me. Theirs is not a quiet celebration; they have lots of fun, in true party fashion.

So how about it? Get your entire family together and plan a birthday party for Jesus. Don't make it a last-minute thing. Put the same time and effort into it as you would if you were planning a family member's party. Decorate the house, and best of all, bake a cake! Make sure the kids help in the kitchen. As you mix the batter and taste the frosting, talk about why we celebrate Christmas. You can even sing "Happy Birthday" to Jesus. Before everyone helps blow out the candles, pray as a family and thank God, who "loved the world so much that he gave his one and only Son" to die for all of our sins.

The Savior—yes, the Messiah, the Lord—has been born today in Bethlehem, the city of David!

LUKE 2:11

80

Get out of the house.

Visit a shut-in, someone who can't drive, and offer to take them out for an afternoon. If they need to run some errands, take them to the store. If nothing else, drive through nearby neighborhoods and look at Christmas lights, and afterward, maybe grab a meal. I love being surrounded by family and friends during the holidays, and I can't imagine how sad I would feel to be alone during Christmas or housebound and unable to drive myself anywhere.

My mom has always enjoyed driving some of the older ladies in our church to the grocery store or out to lunch. Mom is never too busy to spend an hour or more helping. That gift of time is an opportunity to befriend someone who may have no one else to talk to. If you can't think of anyone you know who is in this situation, call your church and ask for a name and phone number of a person who may need a ride here and there.

Let us think of ways to motivate one another
to acts of love and good works.
HEBREWS 10:24

❄ **81** ❄

Give your teenagers the opportunity to shine.

I heard the story of one father who gave his teenage son two hundred dollars and said he should give it to a fellow student in need. The assignment made the teen look a little deeper into the lives of his classmates than he had done before. He knew a girl whose dad had lost his job; she didn't have enough money to buy clothes. The teen knew that two hundred dollars would go a long way to help her, and new clothes would definitely boost her spirits. So the teen entrusted the money to the school's chaplain, who gave it on his behalf—"a friend who just wanted you to have this."

Try this exercise in selflessness with your teenagers. By placing the money in their hands, you are saying, "I trust you." And by asking your teenagers to give the money away, you are helping them become giving people. It could change the way your teenager views the world from that moment on.

They share freely and give generously to those in need.
Their good deeds will be remembered forever.

PSALM 112:9

❄ **82** ❄

Happy day after Christmas.

You know it's coming. You see it on your calendar. December 26. It's the harsh reminder that all good things must come to an end. Christmas Day lasts only as long as every other day of the year. We have twenty-four hours to make as many memories as we can before it's gone. And then comes the big letdown. As far as I'm concerned, the day after Christmas might be the single most depressing day of the year. Time to head back to the shopping mall to return the green turtleneck you got from Grandma. Throw the tree in the trash and take down the stockings from the fireplace. The refrigerator is full of leftovers, and the trash is loaded with discarded wrapping paper. Even the Christmas cookies are getting stale (but I'll still eat them).

What if we didn't let the letdowns win? What if we refused to let the joy of Christmas be packed up for another year? Try fighting off the postholiday blues with this thought: Christmas is the reminder of the hope we have in Christ. And this gift of hope is strong enough to carry us through the other 364 days of the year. So wish people a happy day after Christmas, and when they ask you why, tell them who put that hope in your heart.

Hope in the LORD; for with the LORD there is unfailing love.
PSALM 130:7

❄ 83 ❄

Take Jesus to prison.

Last December I was invited to sing in an unlikely place—a special unit of the prison in Nashville called Jericho. A Christian ministry runs the facility, providing mentors for each of the prisoners, as well as daily devotions. I accepted the invitation, not knowing how much that morning in prison would change me. This concert was like no other I had ever performed. No tickets sold. No lights. No stage. Just me, a guitar, and about 150 prisoners. I was overwhelmed by their genuine appreciation of someone who would take the time to visit them.

At one point I was allowed into the solitary confinement unit. I stood in a cold, empty room lined with two levels of cells. Each cell had a small window. As I began to sing my song "Only Grace," I could see faces appearing in the glass. Talk about an emotional moment! Through my tears, I was reminded that God's grace can bring hope to hopeless places.

Be a part of bringing hope to the hopeless this Christmas. Find out how you can support a prison ministry or perhaps pay a visit. Visit www .givethischristmasaway.com for resources.

Around midnight, Paul and Silas were praying and singing hymns to God,
and the other prisoners were listening.
ACTS 16:25

84

Surprise
the angels.

PROVIDE GIFTS FOR CHILDREN
THROUGH THE SALVATION ARMY'S
ANGEL TREE PROGRAM.

*Do not withhold good from those who deserve it
when it's in your power to help them.*

PROVERBS 3:27

✳ **85** ✳

It's right there in your hands.

I have heard some people say, "Oh, I'll give more when I have more to give." Unfortunately, that rarely winds up being the case. Truth is, if you don't give much when you have little, you will most likely give little when you have much. It had been on my heart for several years to start a nonprofit organization called The History Makers Foundation. I knew this was something God wanted me to do, but I would get overwhelmed by the magnitude of the task and too discouraged to get started. See, I had in my head this great big undertaking of an organization and didn't have the slightest clue of how to get from here to there. It's easy to get disheartened about giving when you feel like what you have is not enough.

But God began showing me the needs of different individuals, and he opened my eyes to see that I don't need some big global operation to accomplish good. That is why my foundation specializes in helping children and families in need, one by one. Don't get so caught up in some grand expectation of how God is going to use you that you miss the everyday ways to give that are right under your nose. Ask God to show you someone in need today whom you may have overlooked. There is no such thing as a small gift in God's eyes.

Do not despise these small beginnings,
for the LORD rejoices to see the work begin.
ZECHARIAH 4:10

Would anyone like a snack?

I love the story in Mark 6 where Jesus takes five loaves of bread and two fish, blesses them, and feeds more than five thousand people. If that isn't impressive enough, there are leftovers! There are many instances when food becomes more than a means of nourishment; it blesses people's hearts too. One man named Dan found that to be true. His wife tells the story:

"Dan received a call from a friend whose brother had been in a serious motorcycle accident. The victim had sustained head, neck, and chest injuries; one femur, driven through his hip, required immediate surgery. Not knowing how long the surgery would take, Dan drove to the hospital, armed with a small cooler of snacks. He found his friend in the waiting room. There were many other family members of the injured man as well (strangers to Dan), gathered on short notice, some from great distances. No one talked much, but the food was accepted gratefully. When the family was called out of the room to talk with the doctors, Dan kept an eye on their things. Though at times Dan felt like he was just sitting and watching a family hurt, his quiet presence and offering of food are still mentioned by them."

He satisfies the thirsty and fills the hungry with good things.

PSALM 107:9

Give an "I love you."

Okay. Florists and chocolatiers might argue that February is the love month because of Valentine's Day. Wedding planners and brides-to-be might make a case for the month of June. (It tops the statistics as the most popular wedding month at nearly 11 percent.) But I want to propose December as our love month. After all, in December we mark the birth of the greatest gift of love to every human being—Jesus Christ, the Son of God.

Here's the plan: every day during December, tell someone in your life you love them. See if you can fill up all thirty-one days with different people. Start with your closest loved ones; that's easy. I enjoy telling my girls—my wife, Emily, and my daughters, Lulu and Delaney—how much I love them. My parents? No problem. My brothers? Yes. Grandparents, aunts, uncles, cousins, friends, coworkers? So many choices. I bet you can come up with way more than thirty-one people. Your delivery method depends mostly on proximity. Face-to-face is best. A phone call works too. (In fact, anytime you talk with someone you're close to, please don't forget to say, "I love you.") Or put a quick note in the mail. Let's get the love flowing!

May you have the power to understand, as all God's people should, how
wide, how long, how high, and how deep his love is.
EPHESIANS 3:18

* **88** *

Read the name tag.

Has this ever happened to you? You've been at an event where you had to wear a name tag. Hours after the event, you're talking to a stranger and suddenly that person calls you by name. *Huh? How do they know my name?* Then it dawns on you. *I forgot to take off my name tag!* Get into the habit of looking for the name tag of every checkout person you see. Then wait for the cashier's smile or startled expression when you actually use his or her name. Calling someone by name is a gift that says, "I'm interested in who you are." Every time you see each other, gather another detail while the person is scanning your soda or counting out your change from the drive-through order.

One woman who started with the name tag connection at the checkout counter says that she now knows that Jill the cashier "has a black Swatch watch exactly like mine though hers is misplaced and needs a battery, plays piano, loves Odwalla juices, prefers cooler weather, and enjoys art galleries." Although it may be against a store's policy for their employees to say Merry Christmas during the holidays, it doesn't mean we can't say it to them. Just be sure to add the person's name. "Merry Christmas, Jill."

She will have a son, and you are to name him Jesus, for he will save his people from their sins.

MATTHEW 1:21

Park in the back.

KEEP CLOSE PARKING SPACES OPEN FOR PEOPLE WHO NEED THEM.

The Holy Spirit produces this kind of fruit in our lives: kindness.

GALATIANS 5:22

Give the reason why.

If you put into practice any of these 101 ways to give this Christmas away (and I hope you do), people will begin to take notice. Folks at the office may be curious as to why you are treating them with such kindness. Your family may see something different in your demeanor and wonder why. A stranger you reach out to might be a bit suspicious about your generosity. Deciding to give this Christmas away means you must also be prepared to answer a question such as "What's gotten into you?"

What would you say if someone asked you why you seem so different? Could you clearly communicate the reason for the joy you have this Christmas? As you give, ask God to prepare you for the opportunity to share your faith with someone who is on the receiving end of one of your acts of kindness. You don't have to come on too strong. But don't hide your faith either. Memorize key Scriptures that you can share when an opportune moment arrives. When your giving generates this kind of response, the value of your gift is eternal.

For God loved the world so much that he gave his one and only Son,
so that everyone who believes in him will not perish but have eternal life.
JOHN 3:16

No gift too small.

God doesn't measure your giving by the dollar amount. He doesn't look down on those whose gifts are smaller than others. He never thinks more highly of the wealthy who give in large amounts, nor does he think less of the less fortunate. Isn't it hard to wrap your head around that way of thinking? Our society leads us in the direction of counting the zeros at the end of a number. As if that tells the whole story. Before rushing to decide whose gift is more valuable this Christmas, remember that in God's eyes, there is no gift too small. Jesus' parable of the widow's offering is the powerful proof that he is not concerned with how much you give, but rather the spirit in which it is given.

Jesus sat down near the collection box in the Temple and watched as the crowds dropped in their money. Many rich people put in large amounts. Then a poor widow came and dropped in two small coins. Jesus called his disciples to him and said, "I tell you the truth, this poor widow has given more than all the others who are making contributions."

MARK 12:41-43

On the twelfth day of Christmas, my true love gave to me . . .

This one is for couples. I'm a songwriter, and oftentimes I'll make up my own words to songs that everyone knows, just to make my little girls laugh. I'll put Lulu's name in a song, just to see if she notices. So here's a unique way of giving Christmas to your spouse. Take "The Twelve Days of Christmas" approach. Work your way from one to twelve, coming up with creative gifts for each day. With each day's gift, include the appropriate lyrics. Here's an example: "On the second day of Christmas, my true love gave to me: two red roses . . ." The gifts don't have to be expensive. Creativity and thoughtfulness score the highest on this assignment. If you're feeling really brave, you can stand up on the final day and sing the complete version of your custom-written song. But try to sing it as fast as you can, because that song takes forever!

Spouses need to know they are more than an afterthought this Christmas. They deserve top priority. Make them feel special. Make it a Christmas that both of you will remember.

Fix your thoughts on what is true, and honorable, and right, and pure, and lovely, and admirable . . . excellent and worthy of praise.
PHILIPPIANS 4:8

❄ **93** ❄
Give your cell phone away.

Cell phones are hot gift items at Christmastime. Maybe you've been hinting that your phone could use a makeover. But what happens to the millions of cell phones people don't want anymore? Tossing them in the trash isn't a good plan. Discarded cell phones account for nearly 65,000 tons of toxic waste in landfills each year! Instead, consider donating the unwanted phone to benefit victims of domestic violence. We know of at least one organization (and I'm sure there are others) that collects unwanted cell phones and gives them to victims of domestic violence to use in emergency situations. Passing along phones has saved hundreds of lives.

My wife, Emily, mentioned it to me because we are getting rid of old cell phones at our house. And while you're at it, what else can you find to give to a worthy cause? Eyeglasses, computers, and empty ink cartridges are among other items that various organizations refurbish for people in need. Visit www.givethischristmasaway.com for more information on how to give your old cell phone away.

Help those in trouble. Then your light will shine out from the darkness.
ISAIAH 58:10

America's got talent. What's yours?

If you've watched television anytime in the last ten years, you've probably seen someone with a specific talent, vying for the big prize. There are talented singers, talented dancers, talented chefs, talented athletes—hey! even talented pets, just to name a few. But have you ever been personally graced by someone's talents, something someone did or made or created that took you totally by surprise? Many people keep their talents under wraps. They don't want to make a big deal about them. But God thinks it's a big deal. He created you with your amazing talents.

So I say, find a way to use your specific talent to give this Christmas away. Are you a writer? Create a Christmas story or poem. Good at sewing? Make stockings or clothes for needy kids. Carpentry? Build the manger for your church's Christmas pageant. Can you whip up hot chocolate? Invite the carolers into your house to warm up. Or keep it within your more intimate circle of family and friends. Pull out your tin whistle when the carols begin. Proudly pass around the plate of cookies baked from your own recipe. Show off the *Nutcracker* dance steps that you've been practicing in your bedroom. Do something that's uniquely you.

> *To those who use well what they are given, even more will be given,*
> *and they will have an abundance.*
>
> MATTHEW 25:29

You never know what a gift can do.

Milton was homeless and living on the streets of Chicago. Every day, a man named Torrey would pass him on the way to work. One day Torrey decided to bring Milton a cup of coffee. That one day turned into every day for over a year. Sometimes T (as Milton called him) would bring his friend food. With each little gift he gave, T always included a promise: "I'll pray for you, Milton."

One day Milton disappeared. T looked for him morning after morning but couldn't find him. He feared the worst. But then, several months later, Milton showed up at his usual location. T almost didn't recognize him. Milton was wearing a suit and tie and held a briefcase by his side. He had come to say thanks. God had used T's love to help Milton see his own self-worth. He had found Jesus through a Christian ministry and been delivered from drug addiction.

When you get the urge to give, don't think twice. Just like T's gift to Milton, your gift to someone else may be the very thing that turns a life around.

The wisdom from above . . . is full of mercy and good deeds.
JAMES 3:17

Learn from vegetables.

WATCH THE VEGGIETALES MOVIE *SAINT NICHOLAS*. YOU'LL LAUGH, CRY, AND LEARN WHY GIVING IS IMPORTANT.

It is more blessed to give than to receive.

ACTS 20:35

Give a friendship a second chance.

Some of us have broken relationships that seem irreparable. Something happened in the past—a quick and thoughtless retort, an e-mail misinterpreted, a gesture unnoticed—that we wish we could take back. But pride gets in the way, and neither side is rushing to an apology; there is only the clash of silence. So how do you make amends and pick up close to where you left off?

Two of my best friends and I had a falling-out a few years ago. We had been meeting every week for prayer and were seeing God use us to strengthen each other. But disagreements damaged our relationship. Consequently, we stopped praying together for several months. But God let each of us know that our friendship wasn't over. We swallowed our pride and reunited, determined to restore what we had had together. To this day, we meet for prayer every Thursday. One friend cowrote my song "The Motions," and the other designed the album artwork. When the devil tries to destroy godly relationships in your life, don't let him win. Give someone a second chance this Christmas, and see how God can mend your broken friendship for his glory.

Love makes up for all offenses.
PROVERBS 10:12

❄ **98** ❄
Compose a Top 10 list.

Give the gift of words by writing down a Top 10 list for someone you love. The list can be the top 10 things you appreciate about that person. Be descriptive and specific. For example, if I were writing down a Top 10 list for my wife, Emily, number 6 could be: "I appreciate how patient you are with me, even though every waking minute of my life is taken up by this Christmas book I am writing." Ha! Get the idea?

After you make your list, don't just stick it in an envelope and hand it to the person. Take a little time, sit down, and actually read it to the recipient. And be sure to make eye contact. You won't want to miss the person's reaction. After all, your words have the power to tear down or build up. Choose the latter this Christmas. Praise and encourage people whom you appreciate. Chances are that you don't pass on enough of those affirmations during the year. When you look over the list, I think your appreciation for your loved one will grow even more. And I guarantee that the person's face will be beaming from all the applause.

Kind words are like honey—sweet to the soul and healthy for the body.
PROVERBS 16:24

❄ **99** ❄

Give with open hands.

I hope this book has provided you and your family with some new and creative ways to give this Christmas. Gifts are important, but *how* we give might be even more so. What fills our hearts not only motivates us to act but also determines whether or not we want to make any real kind of sacrifice. In his book *Red Letters*, Tom Davis provides an insight as to why sometimes we choose not to make a difference: "One reason is because we're afraid. We spend most of our time trying to protect what we have, fearing what would happen if that went away. When we do this, we become shackled to our possessions. In essence, we limit our range of motion. We can't reach far enough to offer compassion because our arms are too busy holding all that we own."

True giving asks us to venture beyond the boundaries of our self-made worlds. It says, "Be willing to live your life with a loose grip on your possessions." So don't be afraid. This Christmas, give with outstretched arms and open hands.

Wherever your treasure is, there the desires of your heart will also be.
MATTHEW 6:21

❄ **100** ❄
Give them a glimpse of Jesus.

There are heroes and superheroes, and then there's Jesus, who out-heroes them all. Have you stopped lately to think about the attributes of Jesus that put him in a category above any hero, real or fictional? Which quality means the most to you? Is it his humble service? his willingness to reach out to broken people? his practical kindness? his personal sacrifice? Maybe it's his gentleness with children or his creative fingerprint on everything in the world. Don't be surprised by the number you'll come up with when you start jotting things down. Meditate on the quality of Jesus that tops your list. Or you can go through your list, day by day, in December. Find a Scripture that mentions each attribute. For example, Hebrews 1:9 says that Jesus loves justice and hates evil. Now here's the part that takes the most work: ask God to help you reflect these same qualities in your own life. Certainly, if you undertake any of the ideas in this book, you are showing people an aspect of Jesus. Pray to become more like him, and give the world a glimpse of the real thing this Christmas.

The Lord—who is the Spirit—makes us more and more like him
as we are changed into his glorious image.
2 CORINTHIANS 3:18

❄ **101** ❄
Fill in the blank.

Give This Christmas Away is all about creating a different kind of Christmas list. Instead of jotting down things you hope to receive, you've just read a list of ways that you can give to others this year. But wait! This is only the beginning. There are innumerable giving possibilities out there that didn't make my list. In fact, I didn't even scratch the surface. So now it's your turn. You fill in the blank. Is there a unique way of giving that you or your family has discovered that brought joy into someone's life? Is there a certain cause, charity, or church project you are especially passionate about? If so, this final idea is all about you. Add to the list by writing on this page your way to give Christmas away. Then join the conversation by sharing with the world your story of giving at www.givethischristmasaway.com.

Now that you know these things, God will bless you for doing them.
JOHN 13:17

ABOUT THE AUTHOR

Matthew West is a Sparrow Records recording artist and an accomplished songwriter who has released three albums since 2002. His latest hit song, "The Motions," stayed on top of Christian radio charts for months in 2009. Matthew has also penned songs for many of today's top Christian and country artists including Rascal Flatts, Billy Ray Cyrus, Natalie Grant, Mark Schultz, and Point of Grace. Among his achievements are two ASCAP Song of the Year awards. He has also been a columnist for *CCM* magazine. Matthew tours nationally, performing 100+ shows per year. He and his wife, Emily, make their home in Franklin, Tennessee, with their two daughters, Lulu and Delaney, and their dog, Earl "The Girl." Visit him online at

www.matthewwest.com

The Power of a Simple Gift

Operation Christmas Child, a project of Samaritan's Purse, brings joy and eternal hope to children in difficult situations around the world through gift-filled shoe boxes and the Good News of God's love. More than 69 million shoe box gifts have been delivered to needy boys and girls, many of whom enroll in our follow-up discipleship program. Pack a shoe box gift this year, and join in the world's largest Christmas project while celebrating the true meaning of Christmas—Jesus Christ.

Additional information:

- To find out more and to order free materials visit www.samaritanspurse.org/occ or call 1-800-353-5949.

- Follow Your Box! Make your $7 shipping donation online, where you can find out the destination of your shoe box gift.

- National Collection Week for shoe box gifts is the week before Thanksgiving each year. To find a drop-off location, use the zip code locator on our Web site. Shoe boxes are accepted year-round at our international headquarters: Samaritan's Purse, 801 Bamboo Road, Boone, NC 28607.